MIRACLES *from*
PRAYERS

"Garden in Iowa with bench seat"

Conversations with God
Dreams
Earthly Angels

ANN MALIK OMAN

Library of Congress Control Number:		2017916873
ISBN:	Hardcover	978-1-5434-6308-8
	Softcover	978-1-5434-6309-5
	eBook	978-1-5434-6310-1

Print information available on the last page.

Rev. date: 11/07/2017

To order additional copies of this book, contact:
Xlibris
1-888-795-4274
www.Xlibris.com
Orders@Xlibris.com
767084

CONTENTS

MIRACLES *from* PRAYERS

DEDICATION

I would like to dedicate this book to all my family members, medical friends, and church members who now rest in peace. May they all be on the fast track to heaven and be reunited with their families. Also my friends from church who helped in the editing of this book: Danielle Glover, Joan Shortino, Fr. Dennis Hadburg, and Joanne Cobb, thank you is not enough. These members of St. John the Beloved are some of the very best our parish has to offer. I love you all most sincerely.

ACKNOWLEDGMENTS

I would like to thank my husband, Jon, and my children, Eric and Abigail, as well as my extended family siblings: my sister, Barbara; Joe, may he rest in peace; and Paul and their spouses, children, and grandchildren. I would like to thank all my friends in the Cobblestone Quilters Guild and the Duck Ditch Quilters. Better friends cannot be found!

Also, I would like to thank all those anonymous faces of caring, compassionate, and comforting people that prayed for me and sent me cards and loving words toward my eventual recovery.

I am also thankful to my church, St. John the Beloved, and Msgr. Chris Latham, Fr. Dennis Hadburg, and the parishioners of our parish.

I would also like to thank my health-care professionals at Palmetto Family Physicians, Charleston Cancer Center, Hollings Cancer Center, Low Country Orthopedic, Charleston Pain Management Specialists, Medical University of South Carolina, Trident Medical Center, and Summerville Medical Center, most especially Dr. McCoy, Dr. Patricia McCuollough, Dr. Frai Liar (RIP), Dr. Charles Graham, Dr. Schmidt, Dr. Holliday, Dr. Back, and Dr. Morasauck.

If I forgot anyone, I am so sorry to have done so, but at the time I needed you in my life, you were there, and that was a gift enough for me.

Why This Book Was Written

When I first went through the first month or so of my plasmacytoma, I was getting radiation treatments. God came to me on several occasions and asked me to write a book for him based on the power of prayer. How was I going to say no to God? I was more than a believer, I was a person who had benefited from prayer. I told God that I would love to honor him by writing a book about prayer and its relationship in my life.

What Is a Miracle?

A miracle is truly a gift from God that you may or may not be praying for, but you know in your heart and soul that because you do not hesitate to pray, God will be more likely to answer your prayers. So never hesitate to pray. You already know God loves you and has mercy on you, and praying is a form of affirmation that you know your prayers will be answered if you have a strong desire to live a longer life and see things that are bound to happen in the future. God heard my pleas and answered my cries for help from him. I was in trouble health wise and knew prayer was my answer to getting well through God's intercession. For me, it was my desire to see my daughter get married and have her first child. Something I am overjoyed to say I lived to see.

I also wanted to see my son have a child, but he and his wife ended up adopting a beautiful seven-and-a-half-year-old that we have all come to love dearly and completely. Today, August 16, 2017, this very same sixteen-year-old is having two surgeries, and we are once again praying that God will guide the surgeons and those of their assisting nurses in the surgical ward. As it turns out, he did quite well during the several hours of surgery, and his anesthesia kept him calm and sedated for quite a while, keeping him relaxed. Later, he was hungry as a horse since he had gone for the major part of the day hungry. More about Christian later in this book.

INTRODUCTION

College days

I received the Holy Spirit into my life on the day of my confirmation when I was in the eighth grade, and I was very touched that day by the power of the Holy Spirit because I am Catholic and I believe that all you have to do is ask the Holy Spirit to help you and he will. So that is how I demonstrated my faith by living my life and trusting in the Holy Spirit.

When I was seventeen, I was in college and got mononucleosis. It was like I was hit by an elephant. I had zero energy. I stayed in the medical center for almost a week while on campus. I had to gargle with a Chloraseptic solution the doctor made for me himself. It seemed to work somewhat anyway. But I was dragging my feet for weeks after being discharged. Mono is brutal to recuperate from. It takes every bit of energy you can muster to get back to a normal existence. It takes months to get to that point.

When I was thirty, I had horrible pain around my upper-right abdominal area and went for some x-rays of that area. My husband and I had a vacation already planned to go to Hawaii, so we went and awaited the results of the x-rays. Upon our arrival home, we discovered that I needed my gallbladder removed. At the hospital, I found out that the doctor also removed my appendix, which had abscessed and was leaking poison into my body, along with my gallbladder. My doctor who performed my gallbladder surgery wouldn't bring me a specimen jar with the gallbladder enclosed because she felt it was too gross to look at and would make me feel sick looking at it. Later, I found out that I could have died from the abscessed organ and could have gotten gangrene.

At the age of forty-seven, I got the blessed event of having kidney stones. It was on Christmas Eve. I went to a Detroit hospital and was put into a wheelchair where I was left to writhe in an assortment of anguish and pain. I felt like I could bend the metal of the emergency-room bed they finally put me in. This was one experience that truly made me want to die. Christmas Eve and Christmas in the hospital in pain, requiring heavy doses of painkillers. My extended family thought I was lying to them because I was missing Christmas. By the following Monday, the urologist put a stint into my urethra, and oh happy day, I had tremendous relief. Although I was bleeding for almost a month, the worst was over. Thank you, Jesus! I never got kidney stones again. I was told to stay away from caffeine and assorted caffeinated food and beverages. At forty-nine, after Jon and I had taken an overland trip to Utah and back, I discovered I had a broken humerus in my right arm. I had been to the MD in July, August, and September; and finally not my family doctor but another doctor told me I needed to wear a sling and wait for the local hospital to call me in for an MRI. My daughter was home from her service time in Iraq, and she and her father were a great help. Well, I also had to make an appointment with an orthopedic sports medicine MD after the MRI, which was set up very poorly for someone with a broken right arm; my orthopedist came to the hospital and chewed out the MRI technician for not supporting my right arm adequately for the procedure. I had to wait a few days to see the orthopedist again, but I sure appreciated his efforts for my comfort. Finally, my appointment had been made, and we had to pick up the films at the hospital to show him how swell my humerus looked. Well, it didn't take me long to figure out that I had bone cancer, and when we saw my orthopedist, I told him that I pretty much figured I had bone cancer. He said I would have to have a biopsy to look at the actual bone and blood and get a clear idea of what we were working with.

Married, Early years with one of my cats/kittens Moe

We'd know in a few days when the biopsy will be done outpatient in a medical clinic. The results were plasmacytoma and multiple myeloma in the bones and blood in my body. Jon and I weren't shocked because we knew we were in God's hands, and he would surround us with the Holy Spirit. We arrived home, so I looked for my American Medical Association Medical Encyclopedia. Once I found it, I looked up multiple myeloma and received a major shock to my entire system. Then I checked the copyright and found that the book was over thirty years old. I asked Jon, "Could you take this book out to the recycling bins? Rip the cover off this book, and throw the remainder into the newspaper and magazine bin."

Jon said, "Okay, but what did you read in there?"

"Well, it said that someone with multiple myeloma in their arm would need to have their arm amputated. That's why I checked out the copyright and saw how old this book was, thirty years old, and decided to toss it out of my house."

It sure was the right thing to do. No wonder, over my life, I had seen so many people without an arm. Imagine myself without a right arm. I cried for what could have been and prayed for those who had lost an arm to multiple myeloma; my thoughts and prayers were with them. That was exactly what I wanted. So at fifty years of age, not only did we celebrate my birthday, I started radiation on the joint of my humerus. I had to have twenty-five radiation exposures, and we were done almost at the end of a month—no weekend treatments. I was very blessed; let the healing begin.

Shortly after my radiation treatments began, a very dear friend and her husband (RIP) brought me a stuffed duck to take with me to treatments. I named him Nipper because he became my close-range defender, along with God. These treatments started out fine; but as the radiation accumulated, I became very tired, slow on the go, and quite fatigued.

I would go to the church services at 9:30 a.m. on Sundays. Then I would sit in the handicapped pew with a hat on my head to hide my baldness and not scare the small children I always seemed to be surrounded. My daughter frequently brought me to church. Lucky me, I got to sit next to Porter; he had his own suffering to attend to, and yet he patted my hand every Sunday and said, "You are going to be fine, Ann."

If only you knew how much that meant to me early on in my treatments. Never a bad word or comment ever came out of Porter's mouth. It was so nice to sit next to him—an earthly angel doing some of God's work. I owe him for the peace of mind he gave me for weeks on end. God blessed me with his presence every week.

25th Anniversary

Prior to the Discovery I have Cancer

CHAPTER 1

Jon and I decided after we retired from our respective jobs that we needed a change from the cold weather of Michigan. Our son, Eric, was living in Goose Creek, so we started making trips to South Carolina and looked at possible options for us as a residence in the Charleston area. Once we became familiar with the area, we started looking seriously at a few locations and made an offer on several houses that were turned down almost immediately. Meanwhile in Michigan, our home was on the market for almost six months before it finally sold. So we were getting anxious to move before the cold weather arrived there. Unbeknownst to us at that time, there was an economic downturn about to hit our area and hit our area in Michigan hard. So we again were blessed to be able to move and get our money out of that house and get on the move.

As luck would have it, we received an acceptable offer on our home in Michigan and sold it in December '03 and then rushed back to South Carolina in November '03 to look at about eighteen houses and found one that would fill our needs. So we made an offer on it, and it was accepted. Once back home, we started packing and making arrangements for movers to pack a few items, pick up the remainder—including my car—and transport everything with the exception of what we could fit into our truck.

The house we had purchased was built in the 1960s and built very solidly with brick on all four sides, including a detached brick two-car garage. We had our hands full with the neglected interior and the yard work. We threw ourselves into cleaning, painting, and updating what we could for many months. After about eight months of Mr. and Mrs. Fix-It Jobs, we decided we needed a break and planned a trip out west. In July, prior to our trip out west, I attended a beach retreat that the Cobblestone Quilters Guild was sponsoring and had a wonderful time. I was working on some small applique blocks at the time and planned on working on more during the trip out west.

Later in July '04, my daughter and I were driving to a fabric store to purchase some items when we were hit from the rear while sitting at a stoplight. There were four vehicles involved in this accident. My car sustained about $5,200 in damages, and it was only a couple years old at the time. Prior to the impact, I was looking in my rearview mirror and actually saw the car that plowed into us, coming toward us at probably 40 mph or more. My only thought was to slam on the brakes harder and throw my right arm out to protect my daughter. Well, slamming on the brake pedal didn't do any good—even though I was five feet or more away from the car in front of me. We ended up under the SUV, and my car looked like an accordion, front and back, from the impact. Thankfully, no one was injured—just damage to property, not bodies. Thank goodness. And thank you, Jesus, for allowing everyone to walk away from this accident.

Abigail and I received a ride to our home from the occupants of the first car waiting at the stoplight. My car was towed to a collision shop to have it assessed as to repairs needed. I was shaken up and unable to call home, so Abby did that for me. I did manage to call my insurance company though, and they sent out the tow truck to take my car away.

A couple of weeks after this accident, I was having extreme difficulty reaching around to my back to fasten my bra. No front-fastening bras for me. But that is what I had to resort to because I couldn't do what I had been doing effortlessly for forty-plus years of my life. I knew something was wrong at that very moment and decided to make an appointment with my family physician.

I went in to see my doctor and was told that my arm had a strained/sprained muscle because of the car accident. Over the next few weeks, I would start to feel better according to my doctor. Right before our trip out west in September 2004, I went back to the doctor and complained that the pain was getting worse and not slacking off one bit and was told to try Aleve for the pain. So that is what I did. Aleve was my pain reliever for over six weeks' time.

Jon and I started organizing what we would be taking out west. We were going as far west as Utah to visit a family friend and her son and also planning on visiting my brother Joe (RIP).

and his family in Missouri on our return trip home. We also had plans to explore the four corners area and the Red Rock Canyons in Utah. So we got everything organized and packed for ourselves. Then we got things organized for our daughter, Abigail, and my cats, Teaser and Moe, so that they would have whatever they would need while we were out of town.

Jon and I were both excited to be taking this very deserved trip. The move and unpacking was so much hard work. All the cleaning and painting had taken its toll. Waiting for contractors to come to install windows and doors was rather time-consuming too. Jon worked on the electricity, and we had electrical contractors put in a larger electrical box. Jon worked on the crawlspace and put in insulation, drainage tiles, and a sump pump.

He also tore down an old metal shed and hauled over fifteen loads of miscellaneous debris, not all of it recyclable to the dump. Whatever we had that was usable went to Habitat for Humanity here in Summerville, South Carolina.

Jon and I headed out west the day after Labor Day and drove through South Carolina, North Carolina, Tennessee, Arkansas, Oklahoma, Texas, New Mexico, Arizona, Colorado, Utah, Wyoming, Nebraska, Iowa, Missouri, Illinois, Kentucky, and then home again.

It was a spectacular trip of gorgeous panoramas, and Jon has the photos to prove it. Although I too took a camera with me, it was difficult for me to hold the camera up high enough to take a proper picture, especially toward the end of this remarkable trip.

While in Utah, we stayed with and visited my dear friend of twenty-five-plus years, Insa, and her son, Kai. It was wonderful to hug them and reminisce. They live in a winter wonderland, Park City, Utah. And Park City is just so magical when there is snow. I had flown out to visit with them the prior February '03 because I just wanted to see my dear, dear friend.

Jon and I completely enjoyed ourselves while traveling and sightseeing. I worked on some applique blocks that I had brought with me as well as some purses that were designed like fish. So I had my creative outlet along with me. Jon and I had wonderful conversations during our travels, discussing what we were going to do when we returned home, planning our next projects with the house. We also discussed where we were headed each day and what we were hoping to see and do.

We were so happy to have Abigail home from her military duty in Iraq, but we knew at the same time that she needed some downtime and to socialize with newfound friends in South Carolina. She had enrolled at the College of Charleston and was taking classes when we left on our trip. We knew she would be busy while we were away from home.

It was so exciting to see so many states while driving through them from one to another. We stayed primarily at Comfort Inns that were very nice, but packing and unpacking gets old pretty quick. We started flirting with the idea of just renting an RV for our next major trip to explore this country. We have not checked into the expenses to travel with an RV, but it is certainly a consideration.

After we had spent about three weeks on the road, we headed toward my brother's home in Missouri and actually stayed at my nephew Jim's home. My brother had his other son, John, and his wife, Stephanie, and their son, Alex, staying with him and his wife, Kay, until their house was finished being built in Missouri.

We all got to visit with each other and see the new grandnephew, so it was very delightful to have that time together.

Unfortunately, my right arm was now to the point where I could not lie in a prone position in bed without using a pillow to prop it up. When I walked, I needed to hold my right arm with my left because it genuinely hurt to have it dangle without support.

After saying our goodbyes to my brother Joe's family, we headed home. But not without telling them all that we loved them and hoped to see them again soon.

By the time we arrived in our new home state of South Carolina, my arm was hurting so badly I had to call my daughter and ask her to make me a sling to put my arm into when I arrived home. I was unable to drive home during this segment of the trip because I could barely turn the ignition switch or turn and steer the steering wheel of the truck. So I knew once again something was very wrong, and I would have to get myself back to the doctor's office for attention.

Abby met me at the door with the sling for my arm when we arrived home. It truly brought me some relief, and I was thankful for it because the pain was very constant now. Using the sling made the pain less painful and a little more bearable.

CHAPTER 2

I called my doctor's office as soon as I knew it was open Monday morning and had an appointment that same day at 11:30 a.m. I was told that the front-office staff would make an appointment for me to have an MRI (magnetic resonance imaging) done that week. I was never hard x-rayed to discover if my bone in my right arm was hurt in some way. I went home and waited for a call telling me of the appointment time for the MRI. By Wednesday, I was getting extremely impatient and upset because I hadn't heard anything back and called them to say how much I was hurting and really needed that appointment this week. Finally, the phone rang, and I was told I had an appointment for that Friday at 10:00 a.m. for the MRI.

I was never hard x-rayed because the belief was that I was just suffering from muscle stress or possibly rotator-cuff pain. Having an MRI would show that area more specifically and profoundly than a hard x-ray would.

Okay, so now, I am waiting another three days for that MRI, and all I am thinking is this pain is awful and I sure wish I had something stronger for the pain than Aleve. I had to just deal with the pain. In other words, accept this pain as with all pain, and take it easy and wait patiently.

Jon took me for the MRI that Friday morning at the Summerville Medical Center. Upon our arrival, we had to fill out the prerequisite paperwork and pay the <u>deductible</u> for the procedure they were performing that day on me. I believe the amount was somewhere between $1,200 and $1,600. That hit me pretty hard because I wasn't prepared for the MRI to cost that amount out of pocket. So I was just a little stunned at that cost on top of the intense pain. I was escorted to the area where the outpatient MRIs were being conducted. I met the technician and was made comfortable on the MRI table prior to the machine being turned on for its job of filming soft tissue in my upper right arm.

I was comfortable because my right arm was propped up and well supported while the filming was being done. Toward the end of filming, the phone rang. The technician answered it and then hung up and told me that the radiologist wanted me to be injected with a radioactive isotope. I've been around for a while. I could figure the radioactive isotope was a pretty clear indicator of a concern; they wanted to follow up what he/she thought was cancer.

I can remember I immediately knew someone suspected cancer in my arm. I also thought that having cancer would certainly explain the pain I was having. So I was injected with the isotope, and more films were taken. When the series was completed, I was told I could leave.

Jon and I met up in the waiting room, and he asked me how it went, and I told him that we had better prepare ourselves for the news that I have cancer because they had injected me with a radioactive isotope. I was convinced that I was going to hear that news shortly. We headed for home, and I started working on accepting the unconfirmed notion that I had cancer. I also started praying very consistently asking God to let this be a curable cancer.

"Give me strength, God. I know I am going to need more of it. Also, help me to strengthen my faith. I know that will also help me get through the days ahead."

We were home the remainder of the day until I received a phone call from my family physician's office asking me to come into the office immediately; it was 5:00 p.m., closing time for the office. So although I thought that was odd, we left for the doctor's office. Upon arrival, I was sent back to one of the examining rooms and given a sling to wear on my right arm. A doctor told me that I had a fracture in my arm and that it was holding on by a thread. I was also told that their office would make an appointment for me with an orthopedic surgeon the following week since it was already Friday evening. They also told me not to carry anything with my right hand in the duration.

The next week, I received the call concerning the appointment with the orthopedic surgeon as well as an appointment for a full-body bone scan at Trident Hospital.

Jon and I went to Summerville Medical Center and picked up the MRIs I had taken the prior Friday and then we went to the orthopedic surgeon's office and dropped them off so he would have them on the following Tuesday to review. Prior to dropping them off at his office though, actually en route to his office, I pulled out the last two films that showed the right arm after the injection of the isotope. What I saw was both frightening and confirming of my worst thoughts. My upper right arm was all aglow, reflecting that it was eaten away by cancer and fractured too. I said to Jon, "I think I really do have cancer seeing these films, and we are just going to have to accept it and deal with it as best we can!"

I knew then that I needed God in my life to a much greater degree than I was currently availing myself. More so than ever before because what I was facing, only he could save me. I also knew I needed to pray as fervently as I knew how and ask God to give me options along the way so that I would not have to face terminal cancer without God's constant presence in my life. So I put all my worries and concerns into God's hands and completely trusted in him to get me through the months, weeks, and days ahead of me. Prayer became my partner to fight this battle ahead of me; I often prayed to the Holy Spirit. When I was confirmed in eighth grade, I remember the impression confirmation had on me. I thought of the Holy Spirit looking after me every day and in every way.

My name is Ann, and I have lived with cancer every day for over ten years. The reality that I had cancer turned into acceptance that I had to work with this setback in order to conquer it immediately. Well, immediately didn't happen because the battle goes on even now. My orthopedic surgeon was struck that I knew I had cancer before he even met me and discussed my MRI, full-body bone scan, and x-ray results with me. He was also stunned that I had already accepted the fact that I had cancer and was ready mentally and physically to fight my battle with cancer. I so wanted to hear that I had options.

Truth is I peeked at my MRI results from about three days prior to my appointment with my orthopedic surgeon before delivering them to his orthopedic office. I knew as soon as I was injected with a radioactive isotope during the actual MRI, that something far more than a sprained or torn muscle was in question. I only needed to see the last two MRIs that were taken to see the ugly truth of the matter. I couldn't drive at the time because I was on very strong pain medication, hydrocodone. Because of where the break was in my right arm, I couldn't be cast; a sling was all they could do for me.

I believed that acceptance would make everything ahead of us easier. Acceptance is empowering and allows you to see things differently. Acceptance brings with it a quiet peace to your heart and soul. Acceptance of the events ahead of us was done with gratitude, faith, and thankfulness.

I prayed like I had never prayed before in my life, and this was not the first stressful crisis I have dealt with during my life. I know everyone doesn't lead an idyllic life and that something traumatizing happens along the way to most all of us. I suppose I had taken my life, family, and friends for granted in some respect until now. Now all I wanted to do is let everyone know what I was going through and just ask them to pray for me and not think negative thoughts but rather stay strong so I could too. I was just reminded of the feeling I would get from everyone praying for me in the morning. When people are praying for you, you will get the feeling of being lifted up and almost floating in your bed, a weightlessness. I mentioned this to Jon often, so I knew many people were praying for us every day I felt like this. There is nothing more special than knowing so many people are praying for you at the same time. And the feeling of elevation in your own bed helped me to get out of bed and challenge myself each day.

It bothered me to no end to have someone I love and care about say that they were afraid, scared, sorry, worried, or that they pitied me. Those are words that are usually spoken by someone who has given up on you, and that is not what I wanted to hear. I felt like this always at this time. So I tried to tell them to take the negative and make it a positive. Instead of being unproductive and dwelling on negativity, please pray and be constructive with their time. That is all I would ask of everyone I knew. And I know many, many people prayed for my cause.

God waits for us to invite him into our lives. I opened my heart to him so that he would enter into my life and share the treasures he had (i.e., blessings and graces) for my life. Trusting in God with all your heart and soul becomes the only way to proceed on a day-to-day basis. Keep your line of communication open with God so that he will direct your path. There are angels all around you in the form of human beings, just like you and me. Often, they give us messages from God, but we are too preoccupied to listen to strangers who stop to talk to us for whatever reason there is in our hearts at the time. God will teach you what love is and to take nothing for granted, neither joy nor sorrow. God appears to us in signs and angels that are all around us; all we need to do is open our minds, our eyes, and our hearts.

I was out shopping with my husband for a piece of fabric at a department store, and a woman in a small motorized shopping cart started making conversation with me. She said to me, "You know you will be all right, don't you?"

And I responded, "Well, I certainly hope so."

And then she said, "Next year (i.e., 2005) would be a very good year for you."

It was at that moment that I realized she was an angel in human form delivering a message from God. A message I had prayed for and received from an earthly angel. I was stunned and overjoyed at the same time. God had sent me an angel to let me know that I would be well again. I was comforted by this God incident, this divine intervention, this Jesus moment, that had occurred. More were to follow.

I know that many, many times I prayed to God for direction, several times a day, so I would know what to do with myself, to not despair, or to become frustrated in my almost constant pain. I learned that nighttime is the toughest time of day when you are facing the darkness with so many questions and concerns in your heart. Emotionally, I could make it through the day because I had two female cats that were my comfort cats. I woke up one day on my La-Z-Boy heavily medicated with hydrocodone and one cat, Teaser, fast asleep on my chest and Moe, my constant companion, asleep on my legs. I woke up, and I was feeling like I had thirty pounds on my chest and legs. I woke and Teaser decided to move on and Moe resumed her regular position lying next to my left leg. They both brought me a certain amount of comfort and love that I needed to mend my body. The darkness tended to make me think of the possibilities I did not want to occur. That is when I prayed as fervently before I went to sleep at night because I knew the devil was working on me to break me of my renewed spirit, strengthened faith, and love for my heavenly Father. And God snapped me out of that pattern of thinking and got me back on the right track. I think that having positive thoughts, a positive disposition, and a positive attitude about every aspect of your life is something that one should pray for and be very thankful for on a daily basis. Having a positive attitude is also comforting to your family and friends.

Prayer became a constant in my life now. Something I made time for because I knew God would listen to my humble pleas for help and strengthen and cure me in time. I didn't know how much time, but I put all my trust in God and prayer.

"Mother and daughter tea at St. John the Beloved"

CHAPTER 3

My religion, Catholicism, has gotten me through the acceptance of the cancer. Prayer and a strengthened faith have also been my salvation in many ways. I have also taken the opportunity to participate in the anointing of the sick, which is a sacrament the Catholic church offers and that also gave me much strength and allowed me to feel closer to my God. Each time I was anointed, I felt renewed in my faith and often cried tears of joy. I was anointed four times during this distressing experience with cancer. Prior to my beginning twenty-five treatments of radiation, prior to my first and second bone marrow transplants, and prior to my annual testing following up on the first and second bone marrow transplants. I was anointed by my parish Monsignor, Chris Latham. I am very happy that I did so. Each time I was anointed, I felt calm and ready to face what was ahead of me. I felt that I was trusting in God to get me through the next thing that I was being faced with. I learned to put my life in God's hands and to accept what would become of my life no matter what that would be.

I must also mention the support of my husband who has been and continues to be an absolute *rock* for me. Strength, courage, and love that I can count on daily to pull me through the emotional and physical lows as they present themselves are constantly available from him, my beloved husband, Jon. He was also known to say, "Just take baby steps, Ann. That is enough for now."

Of course, I had to call my sister and two brothers and tell them that I had a battle ahead of me, but at that time, I didn't know it would turn into such a long war on cancer. All my siblings met my news with confidence that I could beat this beast, cancer, which was growing in my body. My two sisters-in-law were also called by my husband, and they also wanted me to fight this cancer as hard as I could. They all offered me strength, faith, courage, and prayers that gave me more energy to face what was ahead of me in the days, weeks, and months ahead. We also communicated via e-mail to keep everyone that wanted to be updated on my progress in the loop about all the things that were going on with my husband and me during this emotionally and physically draining time. They all promised to pray daily, put my name on prayer lists, light candles at churches, and had masses said with the priest officiating remembering me from the book of intentions.

I also have kept my quilting friends and work friends informed of my health crisis. They all embraced me, hugging me, offering to pray daily for us, offering to drive me to doctor's appointments and to give Jon and my daughter, Abigail, and son, Eric, a break. I don't like to take my family, friends, or health-care professionals for granted so I keep them all in my daily prayers too, and occasionally, I give them small tokens of my appreciation. God is, without exception, very good to us! Everyone in the United States of America is truly blessed, no matter what their personal plight is. Life is not easy; no matter where you are, no one gets away with a rainbow-filled day every day.

The prognosis was that my right humerus ball joint was literally rat eaten. Too explicit? Well, it looked exactly like that description, and additionally, there was a fracture because of the lack of bone to hold the weight of the lower arm. I don't know how I endured the pain for over three months prior to it being diagnosed, but I did. Someway, somehow, God was with me and helped me get through each day with everything that had to be dealt with.

Brother Paul, Sister Barbara and Brother Joe (RIP).

I was so uncomfortable that the only way to find relief was to lie on my recliner or in bed with a pillow under my right arm. The pain became more and more painful every day. I was told I had plasmacytoma in my right arm, which is bone cancer, that was going to test my entire being for everything I was worth. Plasmacytoma is a very fast-growing, very invasive bone cancer. This pain is constant and relentless, and one wishes to sleep through it every time it would hit.

My orthopedic surgeon also scheduled a biopsy to occur after a bone scan and blood work were completed. Before we left his office, he mentioned that if we did not own a La-Z-Boy, we should get one because I would not be able to sleep in a completely prone position in my bed. He also said that if the radiation did not help to eradicate the cancer and allow my bone to start healing, I would then have to have surgery and have the bone replaced with a titanium bone/joint replacement. That was not an option I thought about much because I believed with my whole being that my body was strong and I could heal myself with God's help. I did not take God for granted. I prayed and asked that the radiation would rid my body of the cancer at the site that was being treated. I also asked that I would not have to have surgery and a titanium bone /joint replacement implanted. Jon once again took me to all my appointments. Abigail would come only if she had no college classes scheduled. Eric was busy working full time and not just forty hours per week.

CHAPTER 4

I knew that when I prayed, God would hear my prayers and answer my pleas for strength, healing, a stronger faith, and courage, and I truly believed that I would be cured. I refused to believe there was anything but a cure waiting for me. This whole series of events I was going through was physically, mentally, and sometimes spiritually exhausting. There were days when all I did was pray because I couldn't sleep or just couldn't relax enough to fall asleep. So I prayed. And God answered my prayers. Perhaps he answered my prayers because I would not leave him alone and give up my dream of a cure.

Through it all, I was headstrong about keeping up my sewing and applique projects. I am a creative individual and rarely lack ideas and motivation to bring them to fruition. I tried once a week to use a rotary cutter to cut fabrics for quilting. But I was often disappointed because I didn't have the strength to hold and press down and cut the fabric. It took me months to regain my strength to use an ergonomic rotary cutter, but in January of 2005, I was finally able to use an ergonomic rotary cutter and cut fabric. Jubilation! When I discovered I could do appliqué, I was overjoyed, and at the same time, I was able to be productive and creative with that form of creative sewing and quilting.

I was always thankful to God on a daily basis for the progress I was making. I never doubted that I would make steady progress or waste any precious time getting mad about setbacks. There weren't many setbacks. Just things said that I wished I didn't hear at different moments during this experience. But now, I think that you have to hear the bad along with the good so that you can realize just how far you have come.

By the time I was diagnosed with plasmacytoma, I was simultaneously put on heavy-duty pain and antianxiety medication to keep down the nightmares. I had my share of nightmares prior to starting the antianxiety medication. Usually, the nightmares consisted of enormous bugs attacking me in some bizarre way. Could the bugs have represented the cancer in my body? I had a few rough nights in the interim. I was also having spasms in my right arm until I started these medications, and they were mighty painful, awakening me from my sleep about every hour or so. The antianxiety medication I was prescribed seemed to help these nightmares. A few weeks later, I began radiation therapy but only after completing a full bone scan to check for other sites of cancer within my body. It was discovered that I had a few lesions on my right femur (i.e., upper leg) and my skull as well. We were not going to focus on these lesions until after the twenty-five radiation treatments were over after Thanksgiving 2004. Once my surgery staples were removed from the biopsy of my right arm, I would commence the radiation treatments.

My sister, Barb, came to visit in October '04 and made me a pair of scrub pajamas and a fleece robe from fabrics I had picked out. We celebrated my fiftieth birthday during her visit. My niece, Jeanette, flew down to visit and surprise me for my fiftieth birthday. We had a wonderful celebration with family present. It was all a very big surprise to me, so unexpected at a very critical time for me to keep my spirits up. I will never forget the joy I felt at my party—it was pure bliss for me.

During my radiation treatments, I was doing a lot of applique and keeping myself as busy as I could to distract myself and be productive; at the same time, I was pretty well medicated because of the pain. It is still a wonder to me that I got through such an excruciating first three weeks of waiting for the radiation treatments to start and actually going through the whole series of radiation treatments. I actually do not remember much if anything during that three-week period. When I snapped out of that drugged and sleep-filled time, I was on the mend, and I knew it in my soul that God was busy healing me. I had absolute faith that he would not abandon me and would stick with me throughout the worst of this. I prayed because I knew that if I was "near to God that he would be near to me" (James 4:8). I also knew that if I "cast my burdens upon my Lord that he would sustain me" (Psalm 55:22). People can listen, but only God can heal us.

It is so important to share your need for prayer with family and friends so that God knows that you are loved and needed here and now. I sure had plenty of time to pray daily myself, and pray is what I did and it truly did sustain me. I remember waking up at night and hearing my father's voice telling me, "Don't worry, Ann. This is going to take some time, but you are going to be fine. You are in good hands. God's hands."

I can remember how very happy we all were to have the five-day a week radiation treatments behind us. I think we truly wanted to believe that my battle was over and we could move on from that point; in reality, we were deluding ourselves. Perhaps wanting to deny how serious this health situation was for us. Denial can only allow you a bit of time to think you are better off than you really are. But that was not what we were granted. Another challenge quickly consumed us.

When Jon, my daughter, and I met my radiologist, she had mentioned that she never had a patient of hers survive multiple myeloma. You can imagine how I felt hearing that! Not being a person to cry in public, I waited until we were back in the car, and I just lost it.

In December '04, I went to my oncologist, and he brought up the lesions on my right femur and my skull—much to our dismay. I was secretly praying that they would just disappear on their own or by some miracle God would grant me. What were we thinking? That they would just spontaneously decide to disappear? If the truth be told, I think we couldn't handle hearing more unfavorable news. We were finding it very difficult to deal with any more than one health crisis at a time. Now we had something else to have to accept and deal with. I never lost my faith that God was always with me and would heal me, and that it would just take time. We had the time to dedicate to this whole health crisis, so it was just a matter of hanging in there and believing that God had a greater plan for us.

Jon and I were both retired. Except I was forced into retirement and permanent disability. Definitely not how I would have chosen my future. But the hand of God was in my hand, heart, soul, and I knew come what may, some way, somehow, we would conquer together this cancer; we had a battle to fight and fight we did with the help of our God.

I actually knew about the lesions I had, either because of intuition, a dream, or just a sense of them existing on my bones. When I first found out about the plasmacytoma in my right arm, I recall telling some of my friends that I had lesions on my right femur and my skull. I also remember running my left hand over my head almost daily and thinking that there were lesions on my skull, and then that very notion was confirmed. I wasn't even surprised because I felt that God had already prepared me to accept my lot with the cancer that I now had and all its phases and stages.

I was placed on thalidomide in December 2005 starting with a 200-mg dose but ended up quitting the medication because of a severe rash breaking out on my entire face. I turned beet red, and the skin on my face was absolutely burning and itching. It was brought under control with a cold washcloth and an adult dose of Benadryl. But not fast enough for me to not wish I could tear off my face. I prayed and went to bed, and the rash was gone when I woke up. I asked God to take this discomfort away from me. Again, I thanked God for taking away my anguish and discomfort.

The next morning when I awoke, I wasn't having any problems. I was taken off thalidomide.

My oncologist put me on monthly infusions of Zometa to make my bones less susceptible to additional bone lesions and to harden my bones. When I started my monthly chemotherapy treatments in 2005, I was also put on Decadron to keep me from getting nauseous, Neulasta to boost my white blood cells, Doxil, a long-acting chemotherapy drug, and Vincristine, another long-acting chemotherapy drug. At this same time, we were informed that I had smoldering multiple myeloma, another of the plasma cells chemotherapy, which is a very important part of the immune system. Multiple myeloma is the second most prevalent hematologic cancer (blood cancer) after non-Hodgkin's lymphoma and represents approximately 1 percent of all cancers and 2 percent of all cancer deaths (Multiple Myeloma Research Foundation, Accelerating the Search for a Cure, Current and Emerging Trends in the Treatment of Multiple Myeloma). We could not ignore this development for very long.

Again, I turned to prayer. I knew God would not abandon me, and my numerous pleas for a life without constant pain and also to heal me of this cancer were the constants in my prayers. As always, I prayed for my family and friends and others suffering from numerous cancers that I knew of from recent acquaintance to be blessed and given the help they needed to get through each day.

The oncologist explained the treatment plan, but I think we were both in denial that I had even more cancer treatments ahead of me. We could only handle so much emotionally. Hearing the oncologist then say that he was going to refer me to a bone-marrow transplant specialist really threw me and gave my husband, Jon, pause. I know I wasn't ready to believe that I needed that drastic of measures to eradicate this cancer that was so much worse than I originally imagined. This information made me think that I was in far worse physical shape than I ever dreamed possible. But this, too, I learned to accept. I think it was the initial introduction to what was next on the menu that floored us both. We knew I had osteoporosis, and that is, bones in pretty bad shape—the worst.

We went to see my orthopedic surgeon and my radiation oncologist prior to seeing the BMT specialist MD. The orthopedic surgeon gave me a hug and a kiss on my check and said, "Your arm is healing beautifully. God does good work."

He said I could start physical therapy to get the mobility back in my upper right arm muscles, so I began that grueling process. It was extremely painful, the absolute definition of pain that would not be soothed without strong pain medication prior to and after therapy. I didn't last more than a month with PT because it was just more painful than I could endure; I dreaded it something awful. I knew that I would have to resume PT after I know I am cancer free, hopefully sometime in January '06.

I could only lift my right arm approximately eight degrees. Using a small matchbox car, I was able to run up and down the bathroom wall. That activity really improved my mobility issues as I kept it up for months, and it was not very painful for me.

During January '05, I took an applique class and worked on a crib quilt and started a full-size quilt entitled "At Piece with Time." This quilt became a story quilt of my life. The quilt top is complete, but I have not finished the back for it to be quilted. I do know that I will get this done one day very soon. In March '06, I finished the quilt back, and I am now ready for this quilt to be machine-quilted. It came out beautifully, and I am grateful to the quilter for their attention to this quilt.

During January of '05, I had a dream, and God was telling me that the younger of my two brothers had prostate cancer but wasn't telling anyone. I called my brother the next day and asked him what he was waiting for? He was confused as to what I was referring to. I said, "Listen, I know you have prostate cancer. God told me in a dream."

My brother said he would tell everybody in our family so that they would pray for him.

I said, "I know this is none of my business, but I am worried/concerned for your welfare."

My brother chose robotic surgery at Henry Ford Hospital to eradicate his prostate cancer, and it was very successful along with many, many prayers.

CHAPTER 5

Learning the power of prayer by rededicating myself to God and the Blessed Mother Mary. Accepting what is now going to be my life and the path I will be traveling for probably years to come is really the key to getting through it day by day.

Incidentally, there also was the option that I may need a titanium joint/replacement if my humerus ball joint did not heal on its own. I had never really thought about it that much because I was praying consistently that God would heal my bone with bone and nothing artificial would need to be done. I obviously got my prayers answered. God is so good! Accepting what is now going to be the life path I will be traveling for probably years to come is really the key to getting through it day by day.

While I was going through the radiation therapy in November 2004, I awoke one morning to my deceased father's voice telling me, "Don't worry. You are going to be just fine. It is going to take a while, but you will be fine." I remember that like it happened moments ago. I prayed for a sign that I would make it through everything I would have to endure, and that was my sign: my beloved father speaking to me—how I treasure those moments.

Also while my sister was visiting us in October to early November '04, I awoke early one morning thirsty and got up to go into the kitchen. It was around 4:00 to 5:00 a.m. and still quite dark outside. I looked out onto our patio, and one of the solar lights was blinking on and off as if it were sending me a Morse-code message. The only person I knew that knew that code was my beloved dad. I believe that he wanted me to know that he was near me as I went through this time in my life. Just as I had been with him as he suffered through terminal prostate cancer for five months. A time in my life that I am proud that I stepped up to the base and did all that I could for my dearly beloved dad, including cutting back on my work hours.

My sister was very worried about Jon and me during this first three months. I would tell her and anyone else to please not worry or say they were sorry this was happening to us because worry and saying you are sorry are signs of giving up in my mind. If I am not giving up and willing to fight the battle of my life, then all I want from them is their prayers. I did not want to hear pity in their voices or concerns about how we were managing. We were getting along fine with God's help, and that was enough for us.

This visit was a fine time for us all; we went to the beach, out to eat, and spent time sewing and visiting too. Just the kind of time you want to have with those you love.

Shortly after my sister and brother-in-law headed back to their home in Ohio, Jon had an accident while building me a greenhouse that scared me significantly. I couldn't drive at the time, but our daughter was still home and was able to drive her dad to the doctor's office for a check-up and x-ray. He may have caused or may have already had a pinched disc in his spine because of this fall and was told to take some muscle pain relievers and rest for a week. He did fall on a concrete slab that led up to the greenhouse and is not level, so the ladder was not as stable as it should have been.

Each day, my first prayer is for Jon. "Please, God, bless him and protect him so that he can continue to be my caregiver."

Also in January '05, my radiation oncologist said that she could see that my right humerus was healing very well, but it would take time for all the cancer cells to die off from the radiation treatments I had received in October and November '04. We were satisfied with that explanation. How were we supposed to know that without someone telling us or researching that subject? I had never had a radiologist give me such specifics like that before. I sure did appreciate the honesty and professional attitude.

From there, we were off to the bone-marrow transplant specialist appointment in January '05. We heard several things during this appointment that I don't think we were prepared to hear or wanted to hear for that matter. I kept thinking when am I going to hear something good, something positive, something to give me more hope? It was perhaps too much of a reality check, and this is where we stand. I remember hearing that without one BMT, my life expectancy was two years or less, and I would eventually die of renal failure, which is kidney failure, and is very unpleasant, not to mention multiple bone fractures in addition to kidney dysfunction. I should continue with the Zometa infusions to harden my bones until my time was up.

Then I also remember hearing that my chances of surviving cancer free would be best if I had siblings with matching blood alleles that could donate their T-cells, white blood cells for my two of two recommended

BMTs. But with that type of transplant, Allogeneic, there are bound to be many issues with rejection, leading to possible death of the cancer patient from the BMT process. Although I feared the worst, I still asked my siblings to have their blood tested in May '05, but none of the three were a match. I thought I would feel relieved, but I actually became very disappointed and saddened by that information. I thought, at that time, that a sibling match was my best chance for a full recovery. I did have a deceased sister, Mary Jo, who died of leukemia at age three, who may have been my match, but we will never know. There wasn't time to dwell on the negative for long. I was going to have to go the autologous route for my BMTs, which means I was going to have my own T-cells harvested and use them for my new lease on life twice. I truly believe that I was happy and very blessed that I was able to have another option available to me under these circumstances. Why did I feel like that? Not everyone who gets cancer has options. At that moment in time, I hadn't ever really known anyone who was a cancer survivor of any type of cancer. That is not true today because I know many cancer survivors, thanks to Camp Bluebird, a cancer survivors' camp. Where there is faith, there is hope.

February '05, Jon and I decided we needed a break, and my brother and my sister-in-law on Jon's side offered to have us come and visit them at their winter residence. It was a welcome break from all things medical. In so doing, I had a few emotional moments, realizing all the things that I could not do that everyone else could found me increasingly frustrated during lucid moments. A good time to up my antidepressant medication, which really helped the situation. That was a good decision to get over the emotional setbacks I was having with my medical progress. I began to feel so fragmented. I was torn up physically and was also emotionally becoming detached. I was working on my handwork sewing projects, but it just wasn't enough to make me feel like I was ever going to be whole again.

Patience is so important—learning to take things moment to moment, day to day without apprehension is not easy. But you learn to do it. I also taught myself to pray when I was worried and not waste precious time worrying or crying and being afraid, which I found to be counterproductive and emotionally and physically draining. Also being worried or scared became so unnecessary; I didn't want to waste precious energy on things negative.

I miss driving myself in my own car so very much; it is truly a loss of independence that hurts the most. I know I will be driving again, and that it is not a permanent situation. God will give me back my independence in time. There are many things I have yet to do and many things that my Lord wants me to accomplish, and writing this story of my experience is one of them. At this time, February '06, I am driving again but not for more than an hour or so at a time. There are areas I tend to avoid out of fear left over from my accident. Someday that accident will leave my mind completely.

Praying and being ever so specific in my prayer requests had to be learned over a period. I am what you would call a spontaneous prayer, using memorized prayers interspersed in between my spontaneous prayers. I am constantly praying for a speedy recovery and the end to my almost constant pain. In time, I will be granted what I have fervently prayed for, and that is exactly how things have worked out. I have learned what patience is. Some people never do.

In March '05, I received Neulasta, which was injected to promote higher white blood cell counts from a former deficient count taken during a blood test. This same month, I was especially productive in my sewing room and completed some projects. One was my "At Piece with Time" applique quilt top.

All of the Duck Ditch Quilters organized and sewed me an appliqued duck quilt for me to take to the hospital and to use while I was recuperating at home. Two bone marrow transplants take weeks and months to get back on your feet and life back to normal. I was so comforted by this quilt that everyone had signed the back of, and that meant so much to me too. What a gift!

In 2006, I finished the back for the "At Piece with Time." Also, I completed sixteen applique blocks that was a monthly class called "Flowers in My Garden."

I was taking this specific class at People Places and Quilts, a wonderful effort and a beautiful end product. During the 2006 Cobblestone Quilters Guild Quilt Show, I won an Honorable Mention ribbon for this quilt.

Another quilt I finished was a large wall hanging that looks like a cathedral window and has angels machine-sewn onto it. Again, one of my dear quilting friends machine-quilted this, and it is just a vision for my eyes that buoy my spirit and my husband's spirit. I also started a quilt for the eldest of my two brothers and finished a quilt for a friend's son in Utah. My brother Joe and his wife Kay approved the pattern and fabric choices I had made. I finished the quilt in December '05 and had it machine-quilted by another dear friend of mine so that it could be entered into the Cobblestone Quilters Quilt Show on March '06.

"Flowers in my Garden" quilt.

In preparation for the regimen of chemotherapy I was about to undergo, I had to take thirty steroid pills in March '05 over a three-day time frame, ten pills a day. Since I am not used to taking steroids, they pretty much made me extremely hyper and sleepless in South Carolina for that duration of time. These three days of discomfort made me feel sickly in the head and stomach, a kind of grief that is more than enough to deal with even for the short term. I had to keep praying fervently because I needed to focus on getting better; recovery and not negativity was my constant thought. At this time, I started to be concerned about what I would do if I were alone to battle cancer without my husband's help. Jon's fall from the ladder was still concerning me. Surely, God had no intentions of taking Jon, my caregiver, away from me, not now or anytime soon. I am surely being tested to see if I have what it takes to endure everything that appears and can be overwhelming. One of our supply priests we had at St. John the Beloved said to me that "God wouldn't take Jon away from me as long as I needed him as my caregiver." Such joy I had in my heart hearing that from him.

⊰3◆◆ε⊱

CHAPTER 6

I decided to detoxify myself in March of 2005; yes, just like a drug addict or alcoholic from the Duragesic 50-mg patches I was using to control pain in my right arm. I decided to do it in one weekend and didn't bother using my Ativan/Lorazepam to help me get through that awful self-imposed detoxify time. I literally felt like I should have been sitting in the gutter/ditch outside my home. I was so miserable and then some. But in my mind, I had to get off all this pain medication that was making me feel fairly mentally and physically dysfunctional. That was one of the stupidest things I have done without help from a doctor or nurse, simply because I was compelled to do it on my own. I just wanted off the amount of pain medication I was on at the time. This matter I took into my own hands could have killed me, so do not do what I did.

Why I thought I could do it alone, I still do not know. I think it was a test for me and God to get this done together over the weekend. Well, it worked, but I would not recommend what I did to anyone because I made myself genuinely sick from taking away the Duragesic patch. I had my husband remove the patch on a Friday night and decided to go cold turkey over the weekend and do without it forever after. I spent most of that weekend hiding out in my bedroom, away from bright sights and loud sounds that would make me feel worse than I already felt. I also was dealing with nausea and migraines during that time. I took Zofran for the nausea and Imitrex for the headaches. I didn't have any side effects from either of these medications. Thank you, Jesus, for this help for me at this time.

In March '05, I also started seeing a pain management specialist. And as a result of those visits, I started to receive steroid injections into my muscles in my upper right arm for the atrophy of a few muscles in my arm that needed more physical therapy. The steroid injections helped for a while, but it was only a short-term holiday from the pain. I had to quit the injections prior to going through the preparations for my first bone marrow transplant because steroids would have an adverse effect on the treatments I was to receive.

This same month, one of the members of the Duck Ditch Quilters, who also machine-quilted my quilts for me, made a quilt for me out of South Carolina Quilt blocks that were made by about thirty members of the DDQ group. She decided after she made the quilt with the assortment of blocks that she wanted to give it to me because I was an inspiration to her and a huge motivation to so many people she knew.

I was so filled with appreciation and comforted by this gesture. My heart swelled with the feeling of love that this quilt demonstrated to me. I spent many hours sleeping and napping under the comfort that quilt has given to me.

My sister-in-law Karen and brother-in-law Jeffrey came to visit us on their way home from Florida back to Michigan. My other sister-in-law Nelda from Vancouver, British Columbia, Canada, also came to visit at the same time. It was so nice having them all here to visit and lift my spirits. We were able to attend the Summerville Azalea Festival and enjoy the vendors present and the beauty of the gardens in the park where the festival is annually held.

Left to Right, Ann, Brother-in-law Jeffrey Hamal and
Sister-in-law Karen Hamal. Having fun in Florida sunshine.

CHAPTER 7

During the months of April and May '05 and prior to each BMT, I had chemotherapy treatments; it certainly was not a walk in the park for me physically or emotionally. I experienced excruciating migraines as a result of the initiation of the new intravenous and injected drugs. I also experienced some nausea. Thankfully, I had some very effective medications for those symptoms.

Because of the effects of chemo brain, I would have some difficulty with completing sentences. Jon and I would basically play charades at home to help me complete my sentences and make sense of what I was trying to say. This lasted for a couple of years until my chemotherapy was over. There were many moments when I was unable to complete my thoughts with sufficient words. Keeping at work with it, I could finally speak sentences correctly.

I was not allowed to focus on anything negative for long because we needed to visit the hemapheresis department. Through a very elaborate process, my T-cells (i.e., fresh new baby white blood cells) would be drawn from my blood while at the same time discarding any cancer cells found during this same process. And my red blood cells were cycled back into my body via the chest catheter. The process of harvesting the T-cells took place in June '05 and typically takes a minimum of six hours and up to several days to complete. I was truly blessed to have a total of 21,000,000 harvested in that first six-hour visit, a record breaker. Another miracle! I prayed to the Holy Spirit all that time to stay with me and get me through this process with acceptable results so that I would not have to repeat the harvest for another six hours or more on another day. My prayers were definitely answered. While the pheresis was going on, the director of the lab was commenting to us that "it wasn't looking like we were going to harvest enough in one six-hour time slot." So we had the professional making us think that another day at this would be necessary. I prayed that that would not be the case.

The next day, early in the morning, a technician from the lab called to inform Jon the news of what my T-cell harvest had produced. I wanted to celebrate. But I couldn't do much celebrating because I was admitted to the hospital with an elevated temperature that same day; it was believed that I had contracted an infection. Unless addressed and treated, I could die. So this infection needed to be discovered and stopped. While in the hospital over that weekend, my temperature dropped, and I could be discharged. I busied myself while hospitalized, making yo-yo flowers from circular pieces of colorful fabric. I eventually started making yo-yo bouquets and corsages and gave many of them to thoughtful nurses and other women who had touched my life.

It has occurred to me after much time has gone by that this record harvest of T-cells was also a miracle God worked through me. It was a record T-cell harvest and more than eleven million more than I needed to harvest during a pheresis T-cell harvest. What else could I think? God spared me another day in hemapheresis. He also showed me to trust and rely on him.

The amazing thing to me was that prior to the T-cell harvesting, I was put on Cytoxan to mobilize the stem cells, along with Neupogen (G-CSF) and Leukine (GM-CSF), which are growth factors to mobilize the stem cells as well. After just a week of the GCSF and two days of the GMCSF, I was ready for pheresis with blood counts that were screaming, "Let's go and get this thing done now!" That is exactly what we did and so very successfully.

I knew it was going to happen, and shortly after completing pheresis, my hair started coming out by the handful. A day after starting to lose my hair in that manner, I asked Jon to use our barber set and cut my hair off down to my scalp. It was one of the easier decisions I would be making. I had a cold head in the air conditioning of summer, and once it was fall, I was consumed with the necessity to stay warm in the cooler temps. I received a chemo hat from the chemo lab at my oncologist's office and relied on that rather heavily to keep my head warm day and night; the hat also came in very handy while in the hospital for the BMTs.

I had about a month off prior to my first bone marrow transplant to rest up and prepare myself for what could be a several weeks' stay in the hospital for that BMT. I busied myself during that time with daily prayer, going to Sunday Mass, and planning on and prepping projects to take to the hospital so I would have something to do during good moments. I was admitted the day before my husband's fifty-fourth birthday, and that was particularly tough. I had not been away from him for weeks and weeks and weeks and just did not know how I would fare without his daily support, strength, courage, and love. My reasoning was that I didn't think he should come down to the hospital daily because if I was having a miserable day, I wouldn't be up for visitors, even loved ones. And as it turned out, it was a good plan because it gave him a chance to escape occasionally from the sights, smells, and reality of it all at the hospital and do something he wanted to do in my absence. It became a time for him to renew and recharge himself until I could return home with him.

My sister-in-law, Nelda, came to visit us again from Vancouver, British Columbia, Canada. It was an absolute treat to have her spend time with us at our home. She has such a good attitude concerning how to make it through trying times in your life and also how to stay grounded by relaxing, meditating, and using prayer and your faith in God to get through the tough times. We hated to see her leave because she provided me with an opportunity to talk about my concerns, dreams, and wishes.

The weekend of the Fourth of July 2005, I was attending a Cobblestone Quilters Guild Retreat. It was a very special time for me, a chance to reconnect with colleagues with similar interests in quilting and all things quilting. The retreat was held at St. Christopher's on Seabrook Island, a spectacular place to have a retreat right on the Atlantic Ocean. I was there from Friday to Sunday and really enjoyed the location and myself. It was a relaxing time for my body and mind. I made some new friends and renewed some friendships. It was difficult to leave all that comfort and love I was surrounded with that extended weekend.

While at the retreat, I worked on a needlework organizer and some stuffed Minky bunnies. I have since made five of the organizers and six of the Minky bunnies—all given as gifts or auction items.

No one can tell you just how horrible the experience of being hospitalized long term can be. For my particular situation, I received chemotherapy the first and second days after I was admitted. Melphalan, a very strong radioactive drug that makes any remaining hair follicles fall out in a very short time, was administered intravenously using my chest catheter, which truly was wonderful to have to avoid all the needle sticks. This drug can cause nausea, vomiting, and loss of appetite, and it sure did all that and more to me.

I was able to work on numerous sewing and appliqué projects while in the hospital for the first BMT. I made many yo-yo flower and applique wall hangings and many more yo-yo corsages to give to hospital staff and patients. It felt so good to be creative and productive while feeling so awful at the same time. I often wonder how I did it.

Jon Oman being himself.

Just getting out of bed and doing anything was a huge plus. Prayer was also my constant source of strength during this time. Without my strong faith and my belief that God was there with me wanting me to get well, I could not have endured the emotional and physical trauma my body was experiencing. I believed that God's hand was in my hand.

I also went for walks with a mask on to protect me from germs while my immune system was suppressed. Getting out of my room and going outdoors or elsewhere in the hospital was very good for me physically and emotionally. You feel less secluded when you are able to get out of your hospital room. I happened to be in a quarantined room in the hospital where visitors raise my spirits! There were other patients like myself who were also quarantined and being observed by special oncology nurses and BMT oncologists.

My sister and brother-in-law came to visit us after my first BMT; they visited for almost a week, and I was overjoyed to see them. We had a wonderful visit, went to the beach, out to eat, and my sister and I worked on sewing projects and made meals together. It was the best time. I will cherish those moments I got to share with them both. I made several baby quilts for my niece, Jeanette, who was expecting her baby in September '05. Coincidentally, Laney Ann, Jeanette's first child, was born the same day as my second BMT in September '06.

Unfortunately after that first BMT, I started having adverse reactions to some of the vitamins and prescription medications I was taking. I kept getting a rash on my upper torso that itched like mad, and I had to take steroids, allergy medication, cortisone ointment, and anti-itch lotions to get over this discomfort. I had good reason to pray for this irritation to leave my body. Each day, the rash would lessen to some degree. After about three weeks, I was finally done with it. Thank you, God. Comfort in your own skin is something you don't fully appreciate until you go through an experience like this.

We determined that I was likely allergic to the oxycodone I was taking for the pain in my right arm and the glucosamine chondroitin I was taking for joint pain. I was switched to hydromorphine and quit the glucosamine chondroitin completely.

Another Scare at Home

After some time off between the first bone marrow transplant and the second bone marrow transplant, I was anxious to get the second BMT under way and be able to put it behind me.

During that time off, my husband ended up in the emergency room with an elevated blood pressure, chest pain, and pain in his left arm. What we all thought was a possible heart attack was actually overstressing his left and right arm from pressure washing two days in a row in quite warm South Carolina weather. So he was discharged after an overnight stay and told to slow down and take it easy for the next week and during the heat and humidity of our summer months. Again, I thought, *What would I do without my caregiver?* So again, I had to pause and ask for God's help to get through this. I knew he wouldn't fail me; my faith was strong, and prayer is so very powerful.

Because Jon had to be hospitalized for a day, my dates for testing prior to the second BMT got pushed back a few weeks. My BMT team wanted to be sure that my caregiver was in good enough health to care for me. As it turned out, he was just fine; he and I were however given a good fright that will be remembered for quite some time to come. Now we both realize that although we are only in our early fifties, we are not invincible health wise.

Meanwhile at home, I was preparing for my admittance for my second BMT the end of September '05. I began to pack what I would need for at least a two-week stay at the hospital. Most patients for BMT are told that they will likely be hospitalized for three to six weeks until their blood counts are elevated and temperature is stabilized. One of the things I also completed during my wait for this second BMT was to sew more neonatal blankets for the babies at Medical University of South Carolina. I had also made some blankets prior to my first BMT for the neonatal babies. That project was fulfillment of a promise I had made to God to make these babies' lives more comfortable.

I also felt that I had better get to repotting my collection of orchid plants that I have enjoyed taking care of while anticipating their blooming. In repotting the plants, I doubled the number of plants that I had. These plants are now safely housed in my greenhouse for the colder months with a heater to maintain the temperature and a fan to circulate the air inside the greenhouse. Currently, there are several plants with flower spikes on them so I have some incredible blooms in an assortment of colors to look forward to.

We were told that I would be admitted on September 25, 2005, for my second bone marrow transplant. So we prepared for that day by getting my things packed up so I would have comfortable clothes, favorite pillow, chemo hat, and projects to work on if I felt good enough to attempt something creative.

All that time I was thinking about my first BMT and how hard it was on me emotionally because of being away from home for two weeks or more. I also kept thinking about the nausea, upset stomach, headaches, diarrhea, and just that all-over sick feeling that doesn't want to quit. I knew that I would have to ask God to give me the strength I needed to endure and also to strengthen my faith so that anything that came my way I could get through mentally and physically. Once I found out that I had cancer, plasmacytoma, and multiple myeloma, I knew I had to ask God to forgive me for the sins of disgust I was harboring for several people living and dead in my life. I believed that God would look more pleasantly on my soul if I sheltered no hatred in my heart. These people

I needed to forgive had hurt me severely during my life, and I wanted to write them off with God's help and forgive them so they would not enter my mind in the future. If they did enter my mind, I figured it was the devil working on me so God wouldn't look upon me so favorably. "Banish yourself from my life, Satan," I would say.

Insurance Concerns

We were informed by our insurance company that I was not approved to have a second BMT until six months had lapsed since my first BMT, meaning I would have to wait until January '06 to have a second BMT. At the same time, we were told that we could appeal this decision; that the company (i.e., Ford Motor Company) paying for our insurance had already been documented in their employee medical benefits booklet. My bone-marrow transplant specialist doctor, Dr. Debra Frai Lahr (RIP), with Hollings Cancer Center, and the doctor in charge of approvals at the insurance company talked and agreed that I needed the second BMT during the month of September '05, but it was not his decision alone to make. We needed to appeal to the company paying for our medical insurance to reconsider this second transplant. Within twenty-four hours after initiating this appeal, the second transplant was approved for me. God was looking after me for sure. Following this news, I was then booked for the procedure. I know prayers that I had from family and friends pulled me through this appeal process. I can say with confidence that without the second BMT, I am not sure I would be here to write this testament to the Miracles from Prayer. Since my multiple myeloma was smoldering, I really needed the second BMT very much.

Build Your Life on the Promises of God

The second BMT knocked me around pretty hard. It was not an easy time emotionally, especially when I was told that I would require a platelet transfusion shortly after the BMT procedure was completed. Shortly after I was through with hospital stays and could be left on my own, my husband started to make platelet donations at the Red Cross. It was his way of paying it forward. Each donation of platelets could potentially save the lives of four neonatal babies. He did this for several years until he was found to be anemic and had to take care of his own health. God truly blessed him for his donation of such a precious treasure.

I knew at that very moment that I was at a particularly low point, especially after I found my nurse Renee kneeling next to my bed praying. She told me I had a 104-degree temperature and they were afraid they were going to lose me. I said, "So you took it upon yourself to pray for me."

I guess I was enjoying my extra uninterrupted sleep. I asked her, "How serious was this temperature scare?" and she said, "Serious." Well, I thanked her for her prayers and told her she was a very good nurse. Emotionally, I was thrown into a pretty heavy moment. That fact turned me to God once again. I asked him, Jesus, Mary, and Joseph to stay with me and buoy my spirits so that my faith would not waver or falter.

When I had awakened from this high temperature, I looked up toward the ceiling, and I noticed the angels and saints all dressed in gossamer robes all around the perimeter of the ceiling in my room. It was such a bright white, it was almost blinding. I felt all that better to see that

I was truly being watched over. I knew that I was there for a strongly motivated reason. Life! I wanted my life back, and I did not want to settle for a fully disabled or handicapped future. My prayers were always spontaneous with memorized prayers intermingled. I was thankful for the outlet to peace that prayer offered me.

I had days when I was totally exhausted and only wanted to sleep and pray. I had tremendous trouble keeping food down. Just the smell of food was a terrible put-off to my actually eating any time of the day while in the hospital. I did not even want the food tray brought into my room. Eating soup was one of the only things I welcomed. I also enjoyed eating popsicles, ice cream, broth, and drinking Ensure shakes made with ice cream. Root beer suddenly became a strong craving. One of my nurses actually made me a root beer float, and immediately, I felt wonderful, comforted, and that I could actually make it through another day. Going through all this broadens your life experience. If nothing bad ever happens to you, you are also blocking the good. I decided to share my life with God and my family and dear friends so that I would have the support that only they can offer. I leaned heavily on God, praying almost constantly in the hospital and at least three times a day when I was sent home. I know God's eyes miss nothing and that he knows everything, so I felt free to disclose all my burdens, emotional, physical, and mental to him. I always have felt unburdened after prayer sessions and often enough so to mention my prayers have been answered time after time. I've learned so much trusting in God for all my health needs. I continue to do so even today, 2017.

CHAPTER 8

Upon discharge from the hospital on October 3, 2005, I was home again. Yeah! I was pretty tired and craving food I would never be able to eat at the hospital, though I had little energy to actually spend much time cooking. I was napping for a good part of the afternoon and at least twelve hours at night on top of that. I was catching up on my rest, and hopefully, my T-cell and other blood counts were returning to normal levels. They were just high enough for me to be able to be discharged. During this time, I was very tired and not ambitious concerning sewing projects. We were making plans to get our bedroom painted and carpeted and to remodel the attached bathroom. Everything went well until I developed a temperature on October 7 and had to be readmitted to the hospital to get some control on the infection that was raging somewhere in my body.

My temperature during this time was as high as 103 degrees for over a day. That was a frightening time for me too. I know I was clinging to my faith, then knowing that everything would work out just fine. I hadn't come this far for God to abandon me at such a critical moment in my life. As it turned out, I had no infection, but it took numerous cultures and four days in the hospital to determine that I was just having random temperature fluctuations; who knows why? So home I went. Was I ever happy to sleep in my own bed! I had prayed so much. I felt that I didn't have the energy to pray another prayer. Thinking back, I am sure it was the temperature I was running that made me feel so listless and unable to even pray. It sure was a blessing to know that others were praying for me in my moment of weakness and exhaustion. The remainder of October '05 was spent recuperating from my second BMT and the additional four-day hospitalization. About that time, I received an application to attend a cancer survivors camp, Camp Bluebird sponsored by Hollings Cancer Center. The camp was going to occur on my birthday weekend, November 3–5, and I wondered to myself if I would be up to the task of attending the camp. The camp was called Camp Bluebird, and I was intrigued by the idea of attending the camp and getting away from home and meeting other cancer survivors. I didn't really know any cancer survivors other than breast cancer survivors. I kept thinking how much fun that can be. How am I going to make it through that weekend on someone else's terms?

I was receiving injections of Procrit at the time to get my hemoglobin levels back to normal. By the week prior to the camp, I was still having doubts that I would have the energy for the whole weekend. I even asked my oncology nurse if I should attend the camp. She said I shouldn't miss it! So from there, I thought, *Well, why not?* I filled out the application and waited for a response.

Camp Bluebird was such a joy and not to be missed! I felt like I was united with so many who had experienced what I had. The radiation, the chemo, the steroids, etc., were just a fraction of what these folks had experienced. Although I didn't meet anyone that had battled plasmacytoma or multiple myeloma, I felt so much commonality with these other survivors that it was very comforting and peaceful to me.

I had mentioned prior that to me, being a cancer survivor was all I dreamed of; I would not consider the alternative. These folks all mentioned their connection with God and how their strong faith and belief in God is what got them through their individual battles. We were asked during camp, "Where do you find your joy in your life?"

Many survivors answered <u>God is the joy in their life</u>. I already knew God was the joy in my life, so I answered that having a creative outlet during my bout with cancer was my joy in life. One reason being that by joining in the Quilting Guild and the Splinter group called the Ducks, I made so many new friends. I was able to share my life with so many other comforting and caring people and their families. Being a member of these groups has brought me so much joy in addition to the joy in knowing my God more dearly.

After my birthday in November '05, my brother and sister-in-law came to visit, and by then, I felt pretty good and in an entertaining mood. We had a wonderful visit, cooking, talking, going out to eat, sightseeing, and shopping. I was sad to see them off at the airport. It took me a few days after they left to get out of my missing-them funk. But I renewed my interest in making each day matter and got busy and worked on my applique, machine sewing, and yo-yo making.

For Thanksgiving, our South Carolina family celebrated at my son Eric and daughter-in-law Susan's home. We all did our share of preparing different dishes for the buffet. I remember I brought the cranberry sauce with and without berries. Pillsbury biscuits were also baked off, along with a pumpkin pie with real whipping cream. I provided the makings for two different stuffing: one with nuts and apples and one without, which my daughter Abigail prepared. It was so good to be out of the house and share the holiday with family. Susan's parents were also present for our Thanksgiving feast and brought with them a fried whole turkey, sweet potato soufflé, and their favorite stuffing and gravy.

It was what you could call a huge meal of everything Thanksgiving, and we started off with a beautiful prayer. It truly was a blessing to be together in thanksgiving for the day and the year of blessings.

Shortly after Thanksgiving, I was shopping for muslin fabric to use as applique background and backing fabric for another quilt I was finishing up for the upcoming quilt show in March '06. While purchasing the muslin, a woman I did not know said to me, "You know, you are going to be all right."

And I said, "Well, I certainly hope so."

And in closing, she commented, "Next year will be a very good year for you!"

I was so happy to hear my wish confirmed by what I was certain was an angel in human form. I went dashing off to tell my husband hiding out in the electronics section about this earthly angel in human form.

This earthly angel had confirmed my desire to get a message from God. He sent me an earthly angel, in human form, to deliver his message of faith and hope. I was so happy!

December 2005

My quilting group, the Ducks, had a celebratory Christmas dinner party at an Italian restaurant. We had adopted a family consisting of a grandma and two grandsons. We had made quilts for the three of them out of flannel and homespun and gave them those prior to Christmas. We also collected some money during our dinner out and gave Grandma the cash in the way of a department store cash card. The boys and Grandma were very pleased with their own quilts made with so much love and comfort in mind.

Later that month, I decided to make a Quilt of Valor that I thought at the time would end up at Walter Reed Hospital in Washington, DC. I managed to get it finished over a week prior to Christmas and dropped it off at the collection point. When I saw one of the women in our area in charge of the effort, I asked her if she knew where my quilt ended up, and she commented, "Washington State."

I remember commenting, "Really, that is nice to know," and she further filled me in on the fact that it was now the property of an officer, a spinal injury patient, at the military hospital there. I felt so gratified for having made the effort to make that quilt to comfort that person. I wanted him to know I appreciated his sacrifice for my country and me. Thank you, service members, for your valor and service to our country and all those countries that you come to rescue.

January 2006

I had an appointment with my local oncologist at his office for my monthly infusion of Zometa. About a week later, I was told that my blood work looked really good, and that as far as he was concerned, we would not be adding Thalidomide to my medications because he didn't see where it would benefit me at all. What a relief to know that I would not have to experience adding that to my daily medications. I was definitely allergic to it anyway.

I had an appointment for my first quarterly post-second BMT. I went into Hollings with a twenty-four-hour urine collection (i.e., proteins found in your urine are not good above a certain level) and to have a bone marrow hip tap, followed by a full-body bone scan. Then came the two-week wait for the results of the testing. When I got the results, I heard that my blood counts were very good, and the percentage of cancer cells in my blood and urine were miniscule, not of any significant number of concern. Relief and praise for God's blessings and healing were on my mind for days afterward. I was in my first quarter of remission.

Our family celebrated by going out to eat and toasting to health, love, and faith in God to get us through the moments in life that matter the most. It was a beautiful, thoughtful, and love-filled time with my family here in South Carolina.

Jon had an appointment to see an orthopedic surgeon specializing in hand surgery. Jon needed to have a ganglion cyst removed that was the size of a golf ball. We had put this off for almost a year because of my health-care issues taking priority. Surgery was set for March after the quilt show was over.

Also in January '06, I was approached to participate in a professional video production being done to benefit Camp Bluebird. The video was being made to submit to possible sponsors for the cancer survivor camp in order to solicit funding for the annual camp. We filmed on a Sunday afternoon, and I got to meet a lovely couple that was the video production team. When taping was completed, they both told me that they were struck by what I had to say and that they would be in touch with us again. It was a liberating experience for me to talk about the benefits of attending the survivor camp and hearing and exchanging stories, thoughts, and concerns with others in the same boat.

February 2006

Jon has been working on finishing our master bedroom/bath. We waited patiently while the flooring and walls were ceramic tiled. Once that was completed, Jon started working on the framework for the vanity that he was making for that room. He wanted the vanity to match our USA-made bedroom furniture.

I decided to join St. Vincent de Paul at my church that meets two times a month. We try our best to assist the poor and needy in our community with food, shelter, and financial assistance on their heating and electrical bills. The meetings are handled so well. They begin with an opening prayer, a reading from our handbook, and then we discuss the cases that have been handled and new ones that need attention. Food cards are handed out to those that need them for their home visits and then we make a silent collection to add to our group's money to aid the people we are assisting. It is a very fulfilling group to be a member.

We had made prior plans to travel to Florida to visit a family member and a friend of mine. So we set off on our travels. It was delightful to see their faces light up when they saw how truly well I looked and acted while visiting with them.

During our time in Florida, we went to the Holy Sanctuary to see the gardens and to see the Carillon Tower and to hear the music that emanates from the tower hourly. While just relaxing on a park bench, my sister-in-law Nelda and I were trading pleasantries with passersby. Among a line of visitors to the sanctuary, there was an older woman with a cane who smiled at me and mouthed the words, "Hi. You're going to be okay." And I smiled and said, "Thanks." Again, God had sent me an angel to let me know that 2006 was going to be a very wondrous year for me. Earthly angels in human form are most certainly all around us. We just need to be receptive to them and the messages that they are delivering to us.

I also went to a BYOT (i.e., Bring Your Own Tiara) birthday party for a wonderful person I met through quilting. It was so much fun to wear a tiara and feel so special and regal among friends with like minds. I'm already looking forward to it happening again next year. What fun!

March 2006

When we returned home from our trip to Florida, it was time for the quilt show setup. Jon and I both helped as much as we could with that effort. It was amazing to see all the work that goes on behind the scenes. And being a participant certainly helped to get things set up in record time, knowing that we can appreciate the efforts of all the hands that made lighter work for the people in charge of that event.

Although I entered five items for the very first time in my life in this quilt show, I was thrilled to receive an Honorable Mention for my sixteen-block appliquéd "Flowers in My Garden" quilt. My other entries were judged, so I now have a better idea of what I can do as far as improvement is concerned for future entries. Never overlook a chance to learn.

I was fifty-one years old and one year out of my treatment from multiple myeloma, and much to my complete shock and amazement, I discovered that my head was on fire, figuratively speaking, and it felt like someone was torching my face with a cattle prod. I had gotten shingles right after the 2006 Quilt Show. Believe it or not, I was in a whole lot of hurt. The shingles presented themselves on the right side of my face, eye, and scalp.

I was beyond devastated with this event. The only thing that helped my face and head feel better was applying cold compresses. That day, I had been outdoors and somehow was attacked by fire ants on my foot and my ankle and leg. So I already had a cold compress on those bites. There were about a dozen bites, but they pack a wallop in poison that they love to inject as a defensive attack on predators.

I had been taking a nap on my sleeper sofa just because the ant bites had put a fair share of poison into my system and may have caused the shingles because my body was stressed. All of a sudden, *boom*. All I could do is stomp my feet on the floor and then run to the kitchen faucet and throw cold water onto my face and head.

I really tore the faucet control off the kitchen faucet as Jon can attest to.

When I finally settled down and could figure out what was wrong with me, I called my family physician and received the typical calming lotion and oatmeal bath instructions. Because my case was literally the worst case they had ever seen, they sent me to Storm Eye Institute and they confirmed I was definitely the worst case of facial eye shingles they had ever seen.

Why did this happen to me? Well, the best explanation I know of is I quit my Acyclovir antiviral medication. I was highly susceptible to airborne illnesses and probably should not have quit the antiviral medication when I did.

I received an assortment of eye drops to get rid of the shingles in my eye and had to take them for years in order to obtain the desired result. I suffered from intermittent blindness and low eye pressure (i.e., mushy eye).

From Storm Eye Institute, I went to see a dermatologist, Dr. Germaine, at her office.

She was absolutely remarkable, and she had her assistant put some shots around my eye area on my face where I had the worst pain. She said to Jon and me, "I do not want you to be worrying about anything, absolutely anything. Put everything in God's hands now and for the duration."

After my major bout with shingles, I joined a Bible study group of women from St. John the Beloved which, in many respects, was a way to get a new perspective on approaching the readings and applying them to our everyday lives.

Sister-in-law Kay and my deceased brother Joe.

CHAPTER 9

I suffered through a cyclical occurrence of the shingles for three and a half years. Yes, three and a half years until I found an infectious-diseases doctor that invited my husband and myself into his examining room.

"Shingles, huh," is what he said. "You are in luck," as my eyes shot out of my eye sockets. "I have just the thing for that, an intravenous infusion. It takes two intravenous infusions one month apart, and you should be cured and rid of shingles. You will have to go to Trident in their infusion room, and their pharmacist will make this mixture so it can be infused into your chest catheter."

I had tears streaming down my face before Dr. Morasauk had finished his commentary. I thanked him profusely, and he was happy to be of some help to me. I was thankful to God and for all the prayers being sent up to God for me. Shingles are absolute misery!

So in June and July '10, I was scheduled to have my infusions.

I seldom had a quiet time with the shingles. It was not often because they are able to make you feel that fireworks and sparklers are going off next to your face. Sometimes just a few seconds of relief were all I received by pushing down in the area the shingles had resided. Sometimes the pain was worse, and the pain felt like a flame thrower or just on fire. I heavily relied on ice-cold wash clothes to subdue the awful neuropathy pain I now had to deal with on an almost daily basis, but at night for the most part, it was at its worst.

After the two infusions were over with, I felt better, but I still had post-herpetic neuralgia as a result of having shingles for three and a half years. Now I just had to be thankful because for the most part, I was just tired and sad because of the intermittent shingles outbreaks, amounting to usually one in my right eyebrow area, my right eye, and my scalp.

It's another story clearly with my being totally rid of the shingles. I tried another pain doctor who tried injections of steroids where he thought I would benefit the most and get some relief. Well, that didn't last for too many visits because one day, my forehead decided to inflate like the Elephant Man. What an embarrassment that was. The doctor discontinued the injections because of my negative reaction and stated he had done all that he could do for me. It took days for the inflated forehead to recede but finally it did, and I felt a little more normal looking.

I saw a China-trained acupuncturist with an MD degree because I wanted to see if I would feel any better having acupuncture to make my whole body feel better. I had approximately seven visits to this female acupuncturist, and she was able to help me feel so much better about the assortment of side effects I had. I became more relaxed and less stressed. I would leave her office to head home after an hour of treatment and felt like I was walking on clouds. I wish I could have gone to see her more, but at $70 a visit, it became cost prohibitive quite fast.

At this point, I had gone to visit approximately forty doctors in the area. I ended up going to see a Medical University South Carolina dermatologist next because she could administer injections of painkillers that helped me. One day at her office, she noticed a cyst underneath my right eyebrow and suggested I have it removed. At this moment, I believe I am suffering from another cyst at approximately the same location. The first surgery I had to remove the first cyst, my worry lines went with it. During the in-office surgery, I found the no-sedation method just a little frightening and prayed I could handle that way of removing the cyst. While having surgery, they accidentally hit a nerve, and I think I was plastered to the ceiling for a bit, but it was well deserved. Losing worry lines in the process could be the perk of removing a second cyst in October '17 too.

I was able to see a military MD who transferred to MUSC and happened to be a cornea specialist. My right eye was giving me numerous problems from blindness to limits on my vision and astigmatism because of having the shingles for three and a half years.

He prescribed many vials of eye drops for the scarring left behind by the shingles. Well, that was all well and good until he said, "Your cornea is responding to the eye drops, and I am going to pass you on to a specialist in contact fitting, an ophthalmologist affiliated with Storm Eye Center and MUSC."

The contacts I would be fitted with would resurface my right eye, and I therefore would not need a cornea replacement from a cadaver.

I consider this another miracle on my journey to avoid a transplant interceded by a dear friend who promised me she would do what she could once she was in heaven.

A very dear friend of mine was dying from her third cancer and asked me what she should ask God to do for me. I was so surprised to hear her say that to me. I knew that she was so grateful for my almost daily visits to her home to say prayers with her, my attendance at Mass daily, and remembering her in prayer as well as prayers with her when she was no longer able to talk. I brought food to the family before and after she passed away, a bouquet of red roses, and also a roasted turkey so that the family as they arrived could relax with some tryptophan and be able to get some sleep after their long drives to get to South Carolina. And it worked. I was so happy, and after my dearly beloved friend was placed gently into the ground, she did not waste any time asking God for my miracle. Shortly afterward, I got my answer because the scarring on my eye was indeed going away, and there was no reason to have a cornea transplant from a cadaver in my future. Thank you once again, Jesus. I with the happy heart and joyful emotions.

Left to Right
Dar Guidry, Ann Oman and Barbra Bubnis

If you are wondering, I am the poster girl for shingles, at least around here in South Carolina and among my family. If you haven't gotten shingles yet and have had chicken pox, you have a 1 in 3 chance of contracting them. Nowadays, you can get shingles/zoster vaccine at the pharmacy at the age of fifty. My husband got his shot years ago when pharmacists started doing inoculations. I got vaccinated; in fact, I had to get revaccinated for all my childhood vaccines. Believe me when I say there were many office visits to cover all those vaccines.

I was able to get the shingles vaccine in 2015 at the local pharmacy as instructed by my oncologist and have not had a shingle since. Thank you once again, my Father, Abba, and my Savior.

Around the fall of 2007 to 2012, I started to experience panic attacks and would literally stop breathing; my lips would turn purple and so would my fingernails. I happened to be in church at the time for funeral Masses or regular Sunday Mass. According to the *American Medical Association Medical Journal*, an encyclopedia on helpful medical facts, panic attacks often can begin to show up at a church or synagogue. It was always embarrassing to have this happen because the parish priest would want to call the EMS and have you taken to the emergency room. I did so once, and the ER doctor told me that if this is going to continue when I went to church, then I should stop going to Sunday Mass. My heart and my soul told me I couldn't not go to Sunday/weekend Mass. So I started taking Klonopin two times a day to keep me from panic and to stay calm. At this point of time, there were quite a few friends of mine who were passing away, and they were dying almost every other month. Some funerals I would attend but would have to leave because I was getting nervous and overheated. My ER doctor couldn't give me an explanation for this happening to me. I pretty much figured that it was a stressful time, and my heart was hurting for the families who had lost a loved one. Perhaps I was worried I would lose Jon, and this time of my life was just downright tough on me. Always in the back of my mind, I was concerned about something happening to my husband and I would lose my caregiver. So I was encouraged to pray more for Jon and be thankful to him for my care. He was always asking me if I needed anything or wanted anything or wanted to go anywhere. Thank you, Jesus, for such a loving husband.

I Decide to Start Seeing an Internist, Leaving My Family Physician

The new doctor I ended up seeing on a regular basis—that is, every three months or more often when necessary. He reviewed the records from my prior doctor and noted that I had not had a DEXA bone density test recently, so he referred me to the Women's Center where I could have one done. I went and had the DEXA test, and when I went back to his office after working with the office nurse, Dr. Back came in and so did his physician's assistant and they were discussing my test results from the Women's Center. They said, "What were you told the last time you had that test done?"

I responded, "I was told that I had osteoporosis."

They responded, "Well, your results are remarkable because your bones are normal now."

My response was "Isn't that impossible to go from osteoporosis and bone cancer to normal bones?"

And they both said at the same time, "Ann, it is a miracle that you now have normal bones with what you have been through. This is not something that ever happens, unless it's you!"

"Oh my word, it is a miracle. I never would have expected to happen considering my cancer and all the things that have occurred over the last few years" was my response.

My Beloved Eldest Brother, Joe, Dies on August twenty third 2015

When my brother died, I was not prepared in any way. It wasn't like he had been sick for any length of time in the past. So our family was very surprised and shocked to hear the news. I was thinking who would do the eulogy for him. I didn't know if I could handle that responsibility. It was a big one. Joe always had time to listen to me talk to him about my treatments and broken bones. He was always kind to me and generously offered his Florida house to us as a getaway from home. He and his lovely wife, Kay, were always so generous to me. I was thankful to have them both as part of my life.

So when I was asked to deliver the eulogy fifteen minutes prior to Mass beginning, I was touched and knew that the Holy Spirit would be with me and help me to deliver the best eulogy anyone had ever heard. The church was full, his family was there, his neighbors, as were his coworkers and people he had helped to find jobs during the hard times with the economy. He was a philanthropic man and gave to charity willingly because he had so much. He had built up three businesses and often employed people he knew and never had regrets. He once said to me, "Ann, life is not fair," to my question why is life so hard for me. I understand now; you have to look at everything in life as an opportunity, and even cancer can be something to be thankful for. I learned that people can be more then generous with their treasure, prayers, food, time to visit, and love. So there is a golden lining to everything, even cancer. You need to trust and rely on God for your everyday needs and be generous with your thankfulness and adoration for his answering your prayers.

Author with her Beloved brother Joe (RIP) visiting their Florida home. My hair starting to grow again after treatments were completed.

Sometimes our prayers don't seem to get answered. That doesn't mean we are not worthy. It may be more a matter of we are not ready in our lives for what we are asking for. God is a loving God, merciful and generous with his blessings and graces.

My daughters wedding. Author, daughter Abigail Heidenreich
and husband. We are the proud parents. I made the veil with
tiara and also made alterations to her bridal gown.

CHAPTER 10

I read online at the Mayo Clinic website that if I had strep throat while battling multiple myeloma, the strep throat would eradicate the remaining cancer cells. I had strep throat twice while battling with MM. Each time, I came close to death. I don't know what was wrong with me, but I just didn't want to go to the doctor's office. I felt very lethargic. I had an elevated temperature, and my throat was closing up, making it very difficult to swallow water even with a straw. I was given antibiotics and a shot of penicillin and told to go home and rest. The Mayo Clinic has also engineered a mouse's genome so that their immune cells are genetically engineered to kill cancer cells. Clinical trials that have been completed show that this could be a good treatment for a form of cancer that affects blood plasma called multiple myeloma. There are wonderful things happening in the world of MM because of all the work the Multiple Myeloma Foundation is conducting. They are working directly with pharmaceutical companies.

By the time I reached 2015, I was found to be in remission. My oncologist at that time told me, "I have never had a patient with multiple myeloma survive. So I am going to retire on a high note." Then he gave me a hug and a kiss on my cheek and said I was also his favorite patient. I was overjoyed and again thankful to the Trinity for this remission; I had waited ten years for this. **Miracle**

I am thankful daily for my <u>remission</u>. I know what else could have happened, but I prayed for strength. I saw what happened to other multiple myeloma patients, but I also prayed for them because I could identify with them. I also prayed for a stronger faith constantly.

I believe that there is a cure for cancer in general. But that there is a huge cover-up to not tell or share this fact. Big pharmaceuticals have a lot to lose by not disclosing this information.

It is now 2017, and Jon and I have had a much better life since my going into remission. We now have two grandsons whom we just can't get enough of, and both of our adult children are married and employed. They are respectful, thoughtful, honest, kind, and devoted, and I am proud they are ours.

Jon and I have cruised the Mediterranean in 2015, and this year, we explored the Baltic Sea with a few hundred of our nearest and dearest friends. Both cruises were for us to be with each other and not have to worry about anything, except where we were going to port and what was on the menu for meals all included with our cost of the cruise.

Once home from this cruise, I asked God one evening before going to bed if he would let me have a glimpse of heaven in a dream and he did. I saw my parents looking fabulous in their thirties like honeymooners, my sister who died of leukemia at age three looking absolutely precious, my dearly beloved brother Joe who had died in 2015 a few years ago looking remarkably handsome, and my mother's parents and my father's parents and all my aunts and uncles except one. May they all rest in peace, I miss them all and feel a true void in my heart thinking about their love and devotion to me as a child and a young adult. I know how happy they are in heaven, and that is all the knowledge I need until God allows me to join them there as well.

While in heaven, I was able to talk with my mother's father, my grandpa, and he did not hesitate to tell me that my mother's sister, my aunt, was in purgatory because she did not honor her father in his wishes concerning his inheritance money for his other daughter and his grandchildren. Then he said she would be in purgatory for some time because she broke a major commandment. Because she did not honor his wishes two times: when he died and when she died. He said he had given her explicit instructions concerning the inheritance monies. But she instead did exactly as she pleased without honoring her father. Honor thy father and mother is one of the Ten Commandments. This is a serious commandment, and many children and adults do not honor their parents for one reason or another. If the reason to dishonor the parents is because of alcoholism or drug abuse or something of sexual nature, that is a whole additional story. Apparently, God agreed. Grandpa said I wouldn't see her for some time to come. Dishonoring your parents is not something we should ever consider doing. Because they are our parents and deserve our honor and respect.

I wasn't there long enough to see my deceased cousins or my dearly beloved friend who interceded in getting my cornea repaired, but there is always next time. I told God I was so pleased to see my family members because I have been grieving so long for them. Now I feel like I have received a precious gift from the Trinity because I got a glimpse of heaven and it was glorious! How often does that happen for one of us? What if God were one of us just roaming around and touching believers' lives?

One spiritual phrase I want to remind everyone of is the Trinity. Jesus, God, and the Holy Spirit, the Paraclete, are merciful! And they will answer your prayers if you pray humbly, like a child, and it will be answered in God's time and if it is his will.

Remember, the Trinity is three spiritual beings in one person, so when you pray to one, you are praying to all three.

Surely, I didn't need to publish a book to let my close family and distant ones know how very much I love them. They all made efforts that have put a smile on my face over the years; the good cheer for me from one day to the next was reassuring and a definite boost from God to keep me going. May God bless you, and I wish you the best life you can live, one with God's presence in it.

CHAPTER 11

My beloved grandson, at the age of sixteen, found out that his cancer was back for the second time in his life, September '16. He was five to six years of age the first time around, and he was not adopted at the time. He was in the care of the Department of Social Services and Foster Parents.

Today is August 18, 2017, and he had surgery done on his brain because drainage tubes were impacted and that needed to be cleared or repaired. He was accumulating more fluid on his brain and took to his bed for about a week and a half prior to his being hospitalized because he was so uncomfortable. His surgeries were scheduled for the sixteenth of the month. They had a neurologist and a digestive doctor to do the surgeries. That knowledge gave us all peace of mind and confidence because our boy was going to finally get the surgery he needed.

Christian's surgery was scheduled, and he was sedated, had his head partially shaved, and once asleep, his surgery began at approximately 2:00 p.m. It took approximately two and a half hours. September 2016, we were told that Christian's cancer was back in his brain, and at the base of his spine was a cluster of tumors that would spread throughout his brain. So he had been told that his medulloblastoma was back, and that really hit him hard. He knew so many people were praying for him and that always made him smile. Even with the tumors on his spine, he had no problem sitting and didn't spend time in a wheelchair. There has not been any evidence that he has this cancer to this day.

Either someone told my grandson a pack of lies or all the prayers that have been said for this dear boy have done Christian so much good. I dare say he got his miracle that was prayed for over a year had to go by. It is just unimaginable to me that my grandson had to go through all these, including MRIs quarterly. Nothing being found, but he was having mini seizures and that was another reason for concern; these had occurred for years probably about four years, and he was told he was having indigestion, nausea, and vomiting prior to the mini seizures starting. Well, that really wasn't the case he was having mini seizures for years, but no one wanted to listen. I don't know if hospitals think that the patients are not very medically knowledgeable or what.

Well, this poor young man had to have his drainage tubes from his brain cleaned out/replaced. Now he is looking better than he had for years. He looked anemic for years, and now his complexion is back to normal. He hasn't looked this good for so long, I can only think that God recognizes his faith and devotion to him and the love he has for others, demonstrated by his sharing his possessions with other kids in the hospital. I am so proud of him and his dedication to the happiness of other children who are suffering, and he identifies with them. God bless all the sick little children that God blesses and showers with graces to endure and survive their illnesses and hospitalization. Christian just found out on the 27th of October 2017 that he is cancer free. He had an MRI on the 26th and the department called and said that Christian was cancer free, much to their surprise. Christian received his Miracle from Prayers from his father and God. God sees you and watches over you every day to keep you safe from harm. He loves you and wants nothing more than to await the day you will join him in Heaven. And you will agree it is truly a glorious place to call home.

Grandson Christian at age 6 or so, after his Chemotherapy and surgery. Photo taken by son Eric.

CHAPTER 12

Dear God, please bless Pope Francis, all the priests, sisters, and brothers, and my caregiver and husband, Jon. Bless them with health, joy, happiness, and security. Please also bless my children, Abigail, Eric, Tony, my son-in-law, and Susan, my daughter-in-law, and both of my grandsons, Will and Christian. All the Jager and Heidenreich families. Please bless them all with health, joy, happiness, and security. Please also bless my siblings: Joe, may he rest in peace; Paul and his spouse, Denise; Barb; and their children and grandchildren. Please bless my sisters-in-law, Karen and Nelda, and their spouses, children, and grandchildren. Please also bless all my friends all over the United States who have been praying for me. Please bless all my health-care professionals. Please also bless all my quilting friends in the SC Quilters, Cobblestone Quilters, and Duck Ditch Quilters groups. Please bless all the cancer survivors and volunteers that I met at Camp Bluebird. Please bless our military at home and abroad. Please also bless the hurricane victims and help them to get their lives back together with their families. Please bless the sick and those living in nursing homes and hospitalized so that they can feel your healing and blessings of improved health and love. Please strengthen all our faithful and bless us with your endless love. Please also bless all those in purgatory so that they may be able to get out of purgatory soon.

Candle in marble sand bowl

Hail Mary

Hail Mary full of grace the Lord is with thee; blessed art thou among women, and blessed is the fruit of thy womb, Jesus. Holy Mary Mother of God, pray for us sinners, now and at the hour of our death. Amen.

Our Father

Our Father, who art in heaven; hallowed be Thy name, Thy kingdom come; Thy will be done on earth as it is in heaven. Give us this day our daily bread; and forgive us our trespasses as we forgive those who trespass against us, and lead us not into temptation; but deliver us from evil. Amen

Glory Be to the Father

Glory be to the Father, and to the Son, and to the Holy Spirit. As it was in the beginning, is now, and ever shall be, world without end. Amen

Apostles Creed

Magnificat

Attendance at Daily Mass and Sunday Mass

For me, it is truly important to attend Mass as frequently as possible because of the graces and blessings you receive by doing so. I also try to be a Eucharistic minister if I am needed.

Saying the rosary daily is also a good practice for the faithful to maintain.

Pope John Paul said all five decades of the rosary every day, and he was canonized as a saint recently.

The Chaplet of Mercy

Is also a very good series of prayers to say because it recalls to mind the Passion of Christ to our memories.

The Corpus Christi Rosary

This rosary recalls the life of Christ while he was on earth. It covers his gathering of his disciples and their travels, the parables Christ shared with them, the miracles he worked for the poor, deal, those afflicted with leprosy, hemorrhaging women, paraplegics, bread and wine for a crowd of five thousand plus, and wine for the wedding feast at Cana.

As well as the Passion of Christ, the crucifixion, crowning with thorns, his suffering on the cross, and finally his dying and burial in the tomb donated by a follower of Christ.

The Novena of the Miraculous Medal of Mary

This novena implores the Blessed Mother Mary to hear our prayers and answer our pleas for remembrance of family who are deceased and those who are in purgatory and need prayers to get out of purgatory. It also involves a couple of songs dedicated to our Blessed Mother. This novena was told to St. Catherine Laboure to copy and spread among the believers in the Catholic church.

There are also the Ten Commandments and the holy days of obligation,

Decide to go through a Marian Consecration.

There is a catechism that can fill in anyone with the desire to become Catholic are specific. There are prayers to specific saints and of course have been canonized by a pope that can be prayed to for a multitude of reasons.

St. Jude
St. Peregrine
St. Anthony
St. Teresa
St. Catherine of Sienna
St. Ann
St. Mother Teresa of Calcutta

These are just a few of the saints that you can find prayers to, and they can help you in a variety of ways. If you invest some time in prayer to saints, you will soon find out exactly what I am referring to.

I'm going to make some suggestions as to other prayers you can pray that you can easily find at Catholic bookstores or possibly on the Internet. My personal favorite, the Pauline Bookstores, carries many prayer books that you will find useful on your journey through acquiring a stronger faith and know all the while that your God is a most merciful God.

CHAPTER 13

I am going to make some suggestions that worked for me while making my journey through cancer.

First, drink plenty of fluids to circulate the chemotherapy medications. Stay away from caffeine and sugary beverages. Neither are going to do you any good whatsoever.

I drank broth and tea (i.e., iced teas and Gatorade are a good substitute for the sugary beverages).

Green leafy vegetables and colorful vegetables have lots of antioxidants in them and are also a very good choice to help you stay healthy. Also, many juice manufacturers are cutting back on the sugar they add if any to the natural juices themselves. These products are all natural; read the labels and select wisely.

Fruits and berries in particular are also a very good source of antioxidants because they have very good combinations of vitamins and minerals that you will require to build up your blood and bones.

This is a good time to stay away from sugar and all things containing sugar. But let me add sometimes you just gotta have a piece of cake, and I mean, the creamy, gooey, yummy kind of cake. And once in a while, that is not going to be the straw that will break your back. Try a root beer float; if you liked them before the cancer hit, you should love them after. Just be mindful of what you should stay away from and what is going to do you the most amount of real good, and you will thrive as a result.

Try using plastic utensils for your meals to eat with because you won't get that metallic taste in your mouth if you do so. Worked for me.

I know there is a big argument about eating organic over non-organic. This is where I stand: I truly believe that eating organic is very expensive. My two cancers cost me close to $100,000, and that is without factoring in food. To me, the soil that most farming is done on is already contaminated with arsenic, and that is a fact. So how do you avoid it? Ask a local farmer if they are farming on new land that has not been farmed and if their crops are truly organic. If so, you may be able to get some great items of food from them when it is in season if they are a co-op farmer, and that is a good thing. So give it some thought and do as you can afford. I wish you the very best in your search for healthy antioxidant-full foods.

About the Author

She resides in South Carolina outside of Charleston. This is her first venture writing a book for publication. Having been inspired by God to write this book Her faith and prayer life grew and grew and she began to know the boundaries as God stuck with her and she to get this book about Miracles from Prayers written. She is very proud of her book because she want to inspire more Christians to pray more fervently and frequently to God. God loves and is merciful to all who love him.

INDEX

A

Abigail (daughter), ix, 2–3, 6, 16, 18, 22, 28, 81

Alex (John's son), 5

B

Back (doctor), 68

Barb (sister), 20, 81

bone marrow transplant (BMT), 24

C

cancer, xviii, 8–10, 15–16, 18, 20, 22–25, 30, 46, 53, 66, 69, 73–74, 77–78, 87–88

cancer survivors, 30, 52–53, 81

Christian (grandson), xi, 77–78, 81

Cobblestone Quilters Guild, ix, 2, 32, 42

D

Denise (sister-in-law), 81

DEXA bone density test, 68

Duck Ditch Quilters, ix, 32, 36, 81

E

Eric (son), ix, 1, 16, 18, 81

F

Ford Motor Company, 47

G

Germaine (doctor), 60

H

Henry Ford Hospital, 25

Hollings Cancer Center, ix, 47, 52

I

Insa (friend), 4

J

Jeanette (niece), 20, 44

Jeffrey (brother-in-law), 36

Jim (Joe's son), 5

Joe (brother), ix, 6, 32, 69, 81

John (Joe's son), 5

Jon (husband), ix, xv–xvi, 1, 3–5, 8–11, 16, 18, 22, 24, 28–30, 33, 39, 41, 45, 56–60, 68, 74, 81

K

Kai (Insa's son), 4
Karen (sister-in-law), 36
Kay (Joe's wife), 5, 32, 69

L

Lahr, Debra Frai, 47
Laney Ann (Jeanette's daughter), 44
Latham, Chris, ix, 15

M

magnetic resonance imaging (MRI), xv, 7–11, 78
Mary Jo (deceased), 30
Mayo Clinic, 73
Medical University of South Carolina (MUSC), 46, 65
Moe (cat), 3, 13
Morasauk (doctor), 63
multiple myeloma, xvi–xvii, 22–23, 46–47, 52, 59, 73
Multiple Myeloma Foundation, 73

N

Nelda (sister-in-law), 36, 42, 81

O

oncologist, 22–24, 67, 73
osteoporosis, 24, 68

P

Paul (brother), ix, 81
plasmacytoma, x, xv–xvi, 17, 20, 22, 46, 68
prostate cancer, 25, 28

R

radiation, x, xvii, 15, 17–18, 20–21, 29, 52
Renee (nurse), 48

S

shingles, 59–60, 63–65, 67
Stephanie (John's wife), 5
Storm Eye Institute, 60
Summerville Azalea Festival, 37
Summerville Medical Center, ix, 8–9
Susan (daughter-in-law), 53

T

T-cells, 29–30, 39–40, 51
Teaser (cat), 3, 13
Tony (son-in-law), 81
Trident Hospital, 9

W

Will (grandson), 81
Women's Center, 68